CAREERS WITH

ZOOS AND AQUARIUMS

SOME PEOPLE HAVE A REALLY TOUGH time deciding what they want to do for a living – a career. Your personal interests, talents and how much money you want to make all play a role in making this decision. So do external factors such as how well you do on standardized tests, what programs are available at your high school, and how your counselors, parents and others influence you when you start to think about careers. All of these competing forces can make choosing a career more stressful than it really has to be.

Some careers can be chosen mostly because they are fun. That's right, fun. The practical issues like required education and potential earnings have to be taken into consideration, but how "practical" is it to wake up with a smile on your face every morning because you know you're going to spend your day doing something you really love? Many people burn out on their careers after a few years because they hated what they were doing. What could possibly be better than getting paid to do what you would gladly do for fun?

A career in zoos and aquariums definitely qualifies. Every year millions of people head to zoos and aquariums for entertainment, relaxation and education, and they depend upon dedicated professionals to provide these services. Best of all, increased environmental awareness has made zoos and aquariums more popular than ever, boosting demand for careerists with the right skills to operate them. Do you think you would be happy spending your days taking care of the animals – and people! – at a zoo or aquarium?

You do not have to be a veterinarian to carve out a worthy career in the zoo or aquarium field. Both zoos and aquariums need veterinarians, so you can certainly take that route if you want, but they also need skilled administrators, designers, horticulturists, volunteer coordinators and careerists with standard business and management skills, like marketing and public relations professionals. This report will concentrate on those careers most directly related to zoos and aquariums, however. Careerists interested in veterinary science will find useful information here but should also check out the Careers Report in this series devoted to veterinary careers.

Take careful note of the information you find here. There are sections on how to prepare for your career in zoos or aquariums, what kind of education you will need, how to get a little experience while you are still in high school, and even how much money you can expect to earn at various stages in your career. If you like what you read here, check out some of the organizations listed at the end of this report. You will find even more information about this challenging career, and maybe even a few useful connections. You are making a very important, life-changing decision. You can never know too much.

WHAT YOU CAN DO NOW

THERE ARE MANY THINGS YOU CAN be doing right now to prepare for your career in zoos or aquariums.

Start by taking on a pet or aquarium of your own. If you have chosen to read this report you probably have a keen interest in animals or fish (fish may be animals but for clarity, this report will refer to fish when it means fish and animals when it means other creatures). If you do not already have a pet or two, adopt one. There is no better way to learn about caring for animals or fish than by taking the responsibility upon yourself. If you already have a pet or pets, take an extra-special interest in their welfare. Accompany them to checkups at the vet and ask questions while you are there. If you own fish, try to breed them. If you own a dog, take it to a training class. If you own a cat, love it dearly but do not bother with the training because it will not work. You do not have to deal just with exotic animals in order to learn a thing or two about animals in general.

There is not a zoo or aquarium in the country that doesn't value the contributions of volunteers. So step up and offer your services. Most zoos and aquariums have volunteer programs for interested persons both over and under 18 years of age, so apply to the program that works for you and see what you can get out of it. You may spend most of your time out in the observation area standing around answering the same questions over and over again. That is a necessary function. Animals and fish may be the attractions at zoos and aquariums, but human beings are the customers. Ultimately, zoos and aquariums have to be designed and administered with people in mind. This kind of experience will serve you well later in your career.

There is no better way to learn the ins and outs of a profession or area of endeavor than by reading the trade magazines devoted to it. The Association of Zoos and Aquariums publishes a monthly magazine called *Connect*. Best of all it is available for free online. Read it every month (the link to the association is at the end of this report). You can also check out *Aquarium Fish International*, *Tropical Fish Hobbyist* and *Zoological Science*, among others. Zoos that have membership programs also routinely publish newsletters detailing their latest projects and publicizing volunteer opportunities. Find a few publications that you like and read them regularly.

HISTORY OF THE CAREER

ANIMALS HAVE ALWAYS HELD A special fascination for people. Unfortunately, getting to know them is often difficult. Only a very small number of species have been truly domesticated. Go to the biggest pet shop you can find and count the species. Cats, dogs, fish, birds, a few lizards and reptiles, small mammals and, in an exotic pet shop, maybe a tarantula or a monkey. Aside from farm animals, getting close to any other species requires a zoo or an aquarium. Most people need help from professionals to encounter animals.

Exotic animals are particularly fascinating. "Exotic" is a subjective term but can loosely be described as anything outside your everyday experience. You probably think tigers are exotic. Residents of northern India are more likely to see them as something they have to watch out for when they go into the jungle. Many of the earliest zoos were created primarily to house exotic animals captured somewhere else. This is still true today, although the modern concern with conservation has also created a need to house and care for animals from close to home.

The earliest zoos were known as menageries. Some, like those established in China in about 200 BC, were simply a way to keep many animals in a relatively small space so they could be easily observed or, in some cases, hunted. Animals are purposely hard to see in the wild, but are much easier to spot if they are kept in surroundings intended to make them visible. Ancient Greek explorers brought home animals from around the world, establishing zoos in most of their major cities. The ancient Roman government maintained a large menagerie of animals for use in gladiator games, including lions, tigers and bears, all of whom could be counted upon to give human gladiators a run for their money. Ancient texts record that 5,000 animals were killed in one day to celebrate the opening of the Coliseum in Rome. This kind of spectacle seems shocking today, and would even be illegal in most countries. Our definition of "entertainment" has changed dramatically in the last millennium or two.

Zoos, such as they were, remained the province of the wealthy for more than a thousand years. Private nature preserves and hunting grounds were considered to be worthy adornments to royal estates. Royal families acquired animals from far-off lands through exploration and military conquest. The majority of people lived in a subsistence economy that forced them to see most animals as sources of food or, in the cases of horses and oxen, transportation or power. This is still the case in most of the world. Zoos are of interest mostly in affluent societies where people have the time and money to concern themselves with ideas like conservation.

King Henry I of England founded one of the first zoos to be open to the public in the 12th century. Henry collected a small menagerie of animals and housed them in the Tower of London. Members of the public were able to view the animals for a fee, just like visitors to a modern zoo. There was one difference, however. Patrons who brought an animal to feed to the lions were admitted for free!

The first modern zoo was founded in Paris in 1793, closely followed by the London Zoo in 1828. By this time, Europeans began to take a scientific interest in animals, as opposed to treating them as mere curiosities or game. Zoos spread to the United States shortly thereafter, with major zoos being established in Philadelphia in 1859, New York in 1861 and Chicago in 1868. A few enlightened practitioners of the new science of zoology began to take notice of the plight of some species, and started making efforts to collect, study and breed species in danger of becoming extinct, giving zoos another mission.

Although people had been keeping fish and other marine creatures in ponds for centuries, the first public aquarium was not founded until 1853, in England. Unlike land animals, which can be kept in relatively simple enclosures, sea creatures require much more complex habitats. The problem of putting hundreds of tons of water pressure behind glass was also a problem not solved until well into the Industrial Revolution. Once they were built, public aquariums rivaled zoos in their popularity.

During the 20th century, simple zoo designs featuring cages

gave way to more elaborate and imaginative habitats intended to make animals more comfortable and easier to appreciate. Bars went away and were replaced by moats, ditches and other devices to keep animals and humans safely apart. Zoo design is part art and part science.

Zoos and aquariums have grown dramatically since the mid-20th century. A combination of leisure time and increased environmental awareness has driven demand for zoos and aquariums to unprecedented levels. Most American cities of any size have some kind of zoo or aquarium, and major cities often have large zoos engaged in cutting-edge research.

What qualifies as a zoo or aquarium has also changed with the times. Not so long ago a zoo was a place with animals in cages or confined habitats. Some effort was made to keep the cages comfortable and habitats authentic, but visitors could never forget they were in a zoo. Starting in the 1950s, the American car culture led to the creation of drive-through wildlife parks in which visitors drove their own cars through landscaped habitats to view the animals "in the wild."

Such facilities are rare today but they did lead to the idea of reversing the formula and letting the animals roam while keeping the people in confined spaces. Some of the biggest zoos in the United States are not even zoos in the conventional sense, such as the San Diego Zoo's Wild Animal Park, an enormous adjunct to the regular zoo, and Disney's Animal Kingdom, a theme park that conducts scientific research and promotes conservation.

Aquariums have taken equally large strides. From row after row of small tanks, modern aquariums have grown to encompass aqua parks like SeaWorld, featuring whales and other very large marine mammals. Like Disney's Animal Kingdom, the SeaWorld parks also conduct scientific research behind the scenes. Even their funding mechanism reflects this unusual business model, with theme-park functions expected to make a profit, and research incorporated as a not-for-profit mission. Traditional aquariums have joined in this endeavor. The Shedd Aquarium in Chicago, for example, features a three million-gallon "Oceanarium" for Beluga whales and Pacific white-sided porpoises.

No matter what you decide to specialize in, you are entering this career at a time of strong growth. As entertainment venues, zoos and aquariums are subject to ups and downs in the overall economy. Concern for wildlife and conservation is here to stay, however, ensuring a bright future for zoos, aquariums and the dedicated careerists who make them possible.

WHERE YOU WILL WORK

ZOOS AND AQUARIUMS OPERATE across the United States and around the world. They are among the most popular themed attractions anywhere, along with theme parks and water parks. There is a slight geographical bias toward southern locations, because the warmer weather makes it easier to show animals outdoors, but you should be able to find an entry-level job pretty much anywhere you want.

There is a ranking order in the zoo and aquarium field, however. While you can count on getting a good entry-level job just about anywhere, you may not be able to pursue a long-term career in the same place. Zoos and aquariums tend to reflect the local markets they serve. A zoo in a small city is likely to be smaller and have fewer opportunities than a zoo in a big city. It is simple economics. Zoos make their money by selling annual memberships and admission tickets to patrons. The more patrons there are within driving distance, the more money the zoo is likely to make to fund their operations, including staff. Bigger zoos and aquariums are more likely to be able to offer a steady career progression.

Bigger facilities are also more likely to invest in ancillary activities like breeding programs, community outreach and habitat preservation. Very large zoos, like the San Diego Zoo and Disney's Animal Kingdom, invest heavily in educational programs and projects to conserve animals' native habitats. The San Diego Zoo actually maintains a completely separate, 1,800-acre facility, the San Diego Wild Animal Park, which concentrates on breeding programs. If you are interested in the educational and scientific side of the zoo and aquarium business you should try your best to move up to a big operation as quickly as you can.

Many zoo and aquarium professionals spend time traveling to other zoos and to the various countries their specimens come from. There is considerable trading of animals among zoos. Some zoos have too many lions, some have too few, for example. Many animals are captured in the wild, which requires a very specific set of skills. Some zoos and aquariums participate in conservation programs administered by government agencies and non-governmental organizations. These programs require travel. They may even require you to live in exotic locations for a time.

DESCRIPTION OF WORK DUTIES

Zookeeper

Zookeepers are the foot soldiers of every zoo in the world. Many careerists hold this title for decades, even if their specific duties continually evolve. If your goal is to deal directly with animals, this is the career path for you.

Most zookeepers have at least a bachelor's degree in zoology or biology, although some liberal arts majors have been known to make the grade, as have careerists with no degree but considerable relevant experience, such as growing up on a farm. Entry-level zookeepers may be mostly responsible for cleaning animal enclosures – including shoveling out the animal waste. Senior zookeepers get to do the more interesting and challenging jobs of feeding and caring for the animals.

Many zookeepers specialize in a particular type of animal. Elephants, for example, require very specialized care. Zookeepers who are especially interested in elephants may be assigned to elephant duty and then set their sights on becoming experts on this species. The same can be said for other species that require special skills. Big cats, for example, are potentially dangerous and require highly skilled keepers. Birds come with their own set of challenges and concerns. So do very large animals like giraffes and very powerful animals like rhinos and hippos. Over time many zookeepers develop very specific areas of expertise that they can use to maximize their enjoyment and job opportunities.

Do not shy away from entry-level zookeeper positions just because you do not want to scoop poop. That is like taking a pass on Little League because you only want to play Major League baseball. Zookeepers have to pay their dues, just like everybody else. An entry-level position is necessary for learning and experience.

Aquarist

Aquarists are the keepers of aquarium collections. Just as zookeepers take care of the daily needs of animals, aquarists take care of the daily needs of fish and other marine creatures. Aquarists care for all kinds of sea creatures, from common freshwater tropical fish to exotic saltwater fish and enormous marine mammals.

Careerists who want careers with aquariums often earn degrees in ichthyology, which is the study of fish and marine life. A bachelor's degree is absolutely necessary to enter this profession. There are fewer positions for aquarists than there are for zookeepers, increasing competition for the available jobs.

Caring for fish requires most of the same personal attributes as caring for animals. Careerists in both fields must take their work very seriously, be organized and efficient, and never forget that they have been entrusted with nothing less than the lives of the creatures in their care. On the other hand, fish are not warm and friendly in the way that many land animals or even birds are. Aquarists tend to be more scientifically and technically inclined than zookeepers, who often develop emotional attachments to the animals they look after.

In addition to feeding and otherwise caring for fish, aquarists are responsible for maintaining aquariums, ponds and other marine habitats. This includes maintaining water levels, cleaning glass and other parts of enclosures, and monitoring the chemical composition of the water. Some fish live in fresh water, some in saltwater, and some in brackish water, which is a combination of the two. Additionally, some species need very specific temperatures, PH levels, and other ingredients in their water. Generally, freshwater fish are easier to take care of than saltwater fish. Mixing artificial seawater, for example, can be very tricky.

Veterinarian

If you want to pursue a career as a veterinarian there are many career opportunities available with zoos and similar facilities. Consider this option carefully. You can always change course later and take the more common path for a veterinarian – caring for farm animals and domestic pets. Many veterinarians make careers out of working in zoos because there are so many opportunities there to work with exotic animals they would not encounter anywhere else.

Trainer

Zoos and aquariums have to be entertaining in order to keep bringing in visitors. For centuries people have paid money to see trained animals do interesting and exciting things.

Zoos often have trainers on hand to give shows with animals that respond well to people, such as parrots and monkeys. Few zoos use trainers for big animals like lions and elephants, leaving those roles to circuses, which share some traits with zoos. The most celebrated animal trainers are the aquatic mammal trainers who work with porpoises, dolphins, and whales in aquatic theme parks. Part aquarists and part performers, they get to commune with some of nature's most majestic creatures in a way that most people can only dream about.

There is some opposition to the idea of training animals. Some animal rights activists say the very notion of training animals to do something strictly for entertainment purposes is essentially wrong. Most responsible trainers today concentrate on teaching animals to engage in natural behaviors on command, rather than teaching them to do unusual tricks simply for show. Porpoises and killer whales regularly leap out of the water in the wild. Scientists say they do it because it is fun and it feels good. Today's trainers merely give them opportunities to have that fun while people are watching.

Educator

Educator is a very broad term, but it can be applied to many different positions within zoos and aquariums. All zoos and aquariums justify their existence principally as specialized institutions dedicated to teaching the public about animals, fish and conservation.

Most zoos and aquariums, for example, sponsor educational programs for both the general public and for fellow zoo and aquarium professionals. Behind-the-scenes programs that take visitors to places where only employees usually can go are especially popular. Seminars in the latest developments in conservation or successes in breeding are also high on the list. Children's programs are almost mandatory. Not only are children the hope of the future of conservation, busloads of kids on field trips earn money for zoos and aquariums.

Many zoos and aquariums, and definitely the larger institutions with the biggest research programs, sponsor training programs for zoo and aquarium professionals. These can range from simple internships for college students, to cooperative teaching programs in conjunction with graduate schools, to advanced certificate programs for working professionals. Zoos and aquariums are on top of the newest developments in their fields and make a significant effort to share the latest findings.

Getting into zoo or aquarium education does not necessarily require an education in zoology or ichthyology. Not-for-profit education directors can come from the education profession too. An interest in animals and conservation should be considered necessary.

Curator/Director

Curators and directors – the titles are interchangeable and depend upon the institution in question – are the chief executives of zoos and aquariums. Often veteran zookeepers or aquarists who changed to the leadership track during their careers, curators and directors are ultimately responsible for everything that happens on their watch.

Curators and directors rarely deal directly with animals or fish. Their job is to know what their keepers and aquarists need and make sure that they have it when they need it. This is why most curators and directors start out as keepers or aquarists. By the time they reach the top job, however, their responsibilities have changed entirely.

Like leaders of all not-for-profit institutions, zoo and aquarium directors and curators are responsible for obtaining funding. Partly this is about the activities that obviously earn money, like selling tickets and souvenirs, both of which are important sources of cash flow. At the top level, however, it is about applying for public and private grants, and asking for pledges from wealthy individuals and charitable foundations. This entails attending many black tie events, giving speeches and generally being sociable and persuasive.

Being a zoo or aquarium director or curator may sound like the logical capstone to a career in the field but it's not for everybody. You'll be about as far removed from cleaning cages as possible, but putting on a tuxedo or formal gown and getting money out of people is something that most people aren't very good at. There's no need to set your sights on this position right now. You have decades to go before you're even in the running.

Horticulturist

Most people associate zoos with animals, so it's easy to overlook the fact that plants play a huge role in zoos. Being a horticulturist for a zoo is a varied and challenging career for creative people who care about conservation.

Horticulturists who work for zoos have two main missions: to keep the public areas of the zoo attractively landscaped and to make sure the animal enclosures have the plants they need to look authentic and provide an appropriate environment for the creatures living there.

These are both big responsibilities. Zoos are parks, of a sort. Like parks, zoos need to be carefully landscaped to be pleasing to the eye, and they need to use their space in an environmentally friendly way. Zoos typically feature formal gardens with flowers and other colorful plants along with settings intended to look natural. Plantings can include trees, bushes and groundcover from around the world. Plantings for animal enclosures are even more important. Habitats should look authentic, both for the benefit of visitors who look at them and for the animals who live in them. Some animals may need certain species in their diet, or to build nests, or simply to provide shade on sunny days. Horticulturists have very important roles to play in zoos.

Scientist/Biologist/ Ichthyologist

Scientific research is part of the mission for large zoos and aquariums. They receive grants to conduct scientific research and are in an excellent position to benefit from the newest advances, especially in breeding.

Large zoos and aquariums often employ dedicated scientists on their staffs, working year-round on various projects. There may also be visits by other scientists to the facility, as they make their contributions to the research or just drop by to see how much progress has been made.

Scientists may or may not be veterinarians or ichthyologists in the conventional sense. They could be biologists or specialists in any number of academic disciplines that have some relevance to zoos, aquariums and the creatures in their care. The nature of their specialty may dictate where they can work. They may have to move frequently as money and research moves from one institution to another. They may be expected to perform other functions, such as providing veterinary care to animals, along with their scientific research. If you decide to take this path you should set your sights on earning a PhD degree.

Entry-Level Positions

Zoos and aquariums offer numerous entry-level jobs to prospective careerists. Jobs in the gift shop or volunteer administration office may not seem like they're very important to the caring for animals or fish, but they are absolutely essential to keeping the institution up and running.

Most zoos and aquariums are incorporated as a patchwork of legal entities, some of which are for-profit and some of which are not-for-profit. Most gift shops, for example, are incorporated as profit-making businesses, while most scientific research is not-for-profit. Working in a gift shop or a ticket booth contributes greatly to the bottom line and enables an institution to earn income to support its worthwhile projects.

You will learn something about the zoo and aquarium you are working for no matter what job you do. Working part time in the gift shop for a year or so is also an excellent way to make connections and be among the first to know when career-related positions open up. If you are already on the payroll, you stand a much better chance of getting the professional job you really want.

ZOO AND AQUARIUM PROS TELL THEIR STORIES

I Am a Zoo Director

"You might think my job has mostly to do with animals and conservation. I am a zoo director, after all. The truth is, I rarely work directly with animals or on conservation projects. My primary function is to raise money, not for myself, of course. I get paid pretty well. My job is to raise money for the zoo.

My zoo, like most others, is a not-for-profit institution. We have some for-profit enterprises that contribute to our income, like the gift shops, food stands, publications, and revenue generated by renting out parts of the zoo for meetings, banquets and other events. Overall, however, we are dependent upon contributions to make ends meet.

Contributions come in three types: public, private and individual. Public contributions are those that come from local, state and federal government agencies. We are a leader in scientific research, so we get federal funding, and we are also one of the main generators of tourism for our region, so we get money from local and state governments, too. Private contributions are those that come from private charities and research institutes. Individual contributions come from people – many ordinary people. Everybody likes zoos.

I started out in this field as a zookeeper. I earned a master's degree in zoology and spent a very happy decade working directly with animals. After I gained some seniority I started to move into leadership positions in which my job wasn't about working with animals, but making sure that the people who do work with animals have what they need to do a good job. Along the way I started to earn postgraduate certificates in subjects like nonprofit administration and fundraising, both of which led me to my current position.

I go to many parties and other social events. That sounds like fun, and it usually is, but I mean, I go to MANY parties. I meet and greet, shake hands and give speeches about all the great work the zoo is doing and how we could do more if we just had some more money. I usually get it. At my level, I have to look out for the big picture. I still believe in caring for wildlife and promoting conservation as much as I ever did, but today I pursue my goal in a different way. It took a long time to get to this position, and I've loved every minute."

I Am a Zookeeper

"I get paid to scoop poop. Doesn't sound like a very good deal, I know. But I'm a zookeeper, a junior zookeeper. Somebody has to clean up after the animals.

I've been working as a zookeeper ever since I graduated from college with a bachelor's degree in zoology three years ago. The zoo I work at is fairly small. We have a few research programs, mostly in conjunction with other, larger zoos, and a respectable collection of animals from around the world. It's a good organization and I've learned a great deal working here.

I started out at this zoo working in the gift shop when I was in high school. I thought it was just a low-pressure summer job. I got it because I wanted to get into the zoo for free. After a few months, however, I started to understand just how important the gift shop was to the zoo. The gift shop is one of the few parts of the zoo that actually makes money!

I read many of the books I was selling in the shop, and that job led to my interest in zoology, which is what I majored in in college. I came back to this zoo, which is in my hometown, because they offered me a full-time job while I was still in college.

At a small zoo like this one, we zookeepers get to do almost everything. The only zookeepers who are really specialists are a few of the senior keepers who handle dangerous animals like elephants and big cats. The rest of us rotate around the zoo and get to know something about all the animals. My favorites are the penguins, who are very personable, and the petting zoo, because I can chat with the guests.

This job is as much about customer service as it is about caring for animals. I deal directly with our guests every day. If they're not happy they don't come back. We need them to come back. Without the hundreds of visitors who come here every day, we would have no reason to exist. Some people are against zoos because they think it's wrong to hold animals in captivity. They don't know that most animals held in zoos live longer than their counterparts in the wild, and they refuse to believe that most people just wouldn't care about animals or conservation if they couldn't see animals up-close in zoos. Most people like zoos and we have to do everything we can to keep it that way.

I'll probably earn a master's degree in zoology someday. I could
continue working here with only a bachelor's degree but I wouldn't get very far. This is a scientific profession. I'm in no hurry, but I will earn a graduate degree one of these days."

I Am an Aquarist

"When I tell people that I'm an aquarist they think I'm some sort of fortuneteller. I have to say, 'No, aquarist, not Aquarius.' Both have something to do with water but the similarity ends there.

Like most people in this career, I developed an interest in marine life early on. My first goldfish bowl rapidly turned into a full-blown obsession. A 10-gallon tank soon became a guppy-breeding tank. Some of the guppies were fed to the African cichlids in the nearby 100-gallon tank. Then there was the fishpond in the backyard. Luckily, my parents were supportive and let me set up tanks wherever they would fit. Soon I was breeding tropical fish and giving them away to friends.

I majored in marine biology in college. The major includes some courses in ichthyology, which is the study of fish, but also covers scientific issues related to saltwater and brackish water habitats. I thought this would be a good fit for a career as an aquarist, and it was. I learned all about fish and the habitats they live in. I now specialize in saltwater species, which is much more demanding than freshwater.

I don't mean to knock my colleagues who specialize in freshwater fish. We all have challenging jobs. Artificial saltwater habitats, however, are much more challenging to maintain than artificial freshwater habitats. Saltwater has to be blended and chemicals have to be added to make sure fish stay healthy in small tanks.

I've dealt with all kinds of marine creatures over the years. Most of them have been interesting in one way or another. I get a kick out of the surreal colors of coral-reef fish and find dealing with dangerous species like some eels and rays to be exciting. I've dealt with sharks, but only a little. The only shark species that do well in captivity aren't really very dangerous. They look fearsome, though, and that's enough to keep the guests coming back for more.

Conservation is a big part of why I pursued this career. I haven't spent all of my time working with aquariums. I've had quite a few opportunities to participate in field research at sea. I've gone out in boats for weeks at a time to research fish and marine habitats. There is a worldwide movement to keep an eye on the state of precious coral reefs, some of which are under threat from human activity and erosion. I'm glad to contribute my skills whenever I can. It's one of the many features that make this career so much fun."

I Am an Aquatic Mammal Trainer

"I may be in the photos you took on your summer vacation. If you've been to the famous aqua park where I work as an aquatic mammal trainer you've taken a picture of me. Nobody leaves without getting a shot of me standing on the nose of a killer whale leaping out of the pool. How could anybody miss that?

I majored in marine biology in college and got an internship with an aqua park. Mostly I fed dolphins and seals. It was fun work, and I really liked the animals. Marine mammals are among the most intelligent creatures on the planet. After a while you don't just like them, you get to know them and really enjoy their company. They get to know you, too.

When I was in college I envied the trainers who got to work with the killer whales. Despite the name, killer whales are actually quite gentle with their trusted trainers. As long as they are fed on time! Trainers work very closely with the whales to teach them to perform natural behaviors on command. Killer whales really do breach the water in the wild. They are happy to jump through hoops and do other things to make those natural behaviors entertaining to the public. In fact, they look forward to it.

I worked my way up to becoming an aquatic mammal trainer by working hard and being very tenacious. The final choice is actually made by the whales themselves. Like people, they won't work very well with people they don't like. Trainers need the résumé and experience to get an interview with the human employers at the aqua park, but the whales make the final decision.

I can't tell you how much I love my job. I get to do four shows a day with my best friends in the world. We have a pod of three whales here and eight full-time trainers. We all rotate our shifts during the course of a typical week so we can maintain our working relationships with the whales and don't get worn out by the performances. Doing a show is like competing in a swim meet, but for half an hour straight. You have to be in great shape to do this job. This is the kind of job nobody could do forever because it's too physically demanding. But it is one of the world's coolest jobs. I'll do it for as long as the whales let me."

I Am a Zoologist

"I always wanted to work with animals but was never very interested in conventional zoo keeping. I liked visiting the zoo, but I've always had a scientific mind. I settled upon zoology as an undergraduate in college and worked my way up to a PhD degree. I get to spend my days conducting scientific research on very interesting animals.

Something that most people don't realize is that zoos are a very important part of the scientific community. Most people see zoos as a form of entertainment and recreation. They are, but they are so much more. In my career I have worked for both zoos and universities although you'd be hard-pressed to tell the difference. I've spent most of my time at zoos, even when I've been on a university payroll.

Zoos have features that are beneficial to zoologists, like

enclosures for animals, and staffs of zookeepers to look after them. We couldn't do our work without zoos. We do research in the wild, which is always interesting and productive, but where would we take animals we bring home if it weren't for zoos? I don't even know.

During my career I've seen many changes, and they've all been for the better. Widespread awareness of conservation and the need to be environmentally friendly have dramatically improved the state of zoos and of wilderness habitats. National parks in this country and around the world are booming to a degree I never could have predicted when I got into this career. All of this has made my job simultaneously easier and more demanding. Easier because there's more funding available than ever before, and more demanding because so many more people are interested in what I do.

I've also been very heartened to see the growth in high-volume theme parks that promote conservation and make money doing it. They're doing a great job at influencing the decisions people make about conservation, and they reinvest their profits in research like I am doing. This is something else I never would have predicted a few decades ago. Contributions are great but if we can generate money through actual commercial profit, so much the better.

Zoology is a great career for people who are prepared to dedicate their lives to it. Science is a never-ending pursuit of knowledge. If zoology is your passion, you'll be very happy."

PERSONAL QUALIFICATIONS

MANY, MANY PEOPLE WANT TO GET into a zoo and aquarium career. People with an interest in this work tend not to want to do anything else, which makes competition keen, especially for the top jobs.

You are probably reading this report because you have a sincere interest in wildlife, conservation and the environment. You will need it if you want to succeed in zoos and aquariums. You do not need to be a passionate animal rights fanatic – in fact, many of them disapprove of zoos – but you do need to understand that living creatures are not simply objects to be displayed like the artifacts in a museum. They require delicate care, proper feeding and comfortable habitats. They deserve to be treated with respect. This should seem natural to you.

Zoos and aquariums may be fun destinations for visitors, but their primary purpose is educational. The whole idea is to get up close and personal with creatures you do not see every day. Most zoos and aquariums collect critters from exotic locations most people are not likely to visit on their own. It is hard to get ordinary people to care much about species they have never encountered. That is why zoos and aquariums take an educational angle on everything they do, from the interpretive signs in front of enclosures telling you everything you ever wanted to know about the creatures you are looking at, to more structured educational programs that require time spent in traditional classrooms. You should learn basic teaching skills. You should be able to give a good lecture or informative talk, at least.

No matter how dedicated you are to animals and conservation, it helps to be a realist when it comes to the modern business of zoos and aquariums. Most such facilities are a combination of for-profit and not-for-profit enterprises carefully balanced to keep the whole organization economically viable. Zoos and aquariums make money from membership and ticket sales, publications, and the gift shop, but they also have to solicit donations and apply for grants in order to pay the bills. These requests for money run up against other competing needs in the community and are sometimes considered not as necessary.

Zoos are also in the middle of an impassioned debate about the proper treatment of animals. Some people think that animals should never be held in captivity, no matter how humane their treatment. Others tend to agree but argue that a few animals need to be displayed in zoos in order to enhance awareness of endangered species and the importance of conservation. Advocates of species preservation see zoos as a last ditch effort to keep threatened species from becoming extinct by breeding and housing specimens. If you enter this line of work you will become an advocate of some position with the financial and ethical debates.

ATTRACTIVE FEATURES

NOT SURPRISINGLY THERE IS MUCH TO like about a career in zoos or aquariums. It is a perfect example of a career that attracts people who have never wanted to do anything else. If you enter this career you will not acquire a conventional set of skills easily transferred to other industries. You will spend relatively little time sitting behind a desk in an office. You will do things most people do not understand. You probably will not give it much thought because you have never wanted to do anything else. Like most people who go into this line of work, you were probably captivated by the animal world as a kid, and have dreamed of spending your working life in it ever since.

You have probably guessed that you will get to spend much of your working time with animals. You will get discounts at the gift shop and in the restaurant. What about opportunities to travel and participate in scientific projects all over the world? Depending upon exactly what route you take into your zoo or aquarium career you could find yourself doing both. The part of zoos and aquariums that most people see is just the public face of the organization that justifies everything that goes on behind the scenes. These projects are where zoos make their contributions to conservation and wildlife. These projects could not be undertaken without the financial support provided by members and visitors. Perhaps the best feature of all is the fact that you will be paid to do something that most people have to relegate to weekends or vacations. Zoos, aquariums and theme parks are places that people go to have fun. Maybe you have wondered how cool it would be to spend your working life there. You can be one of the lucky few who actually do.

UNATTRACTIVE FEATURES

NOT EVERYONE THINKS ZOOS AND aquariums are as wonderful as you do. Go to a major aquarium or aquatic park, especially a very large one with marine mammals like dolphins and whales, and you may see placard-carrying protesters on the streets outside. The same goes for zoos, especially when they acquire a particularly exotic new animal, open a new attraction sure to attract a few reporters, or reveal the death of an animal, even if through completely natural causes. Many in the animal rights movement believe strongly that zoos and aquariums are little more than prisons for the animals and fish entrapped in them. There is no denying that they have a point, and modern zoos, in particular, have made great efforts to house animals in large, lifelike surroundings rather than the cramped cages of the past. Your argument will be that without zoos and aquariums most people would have no contact with any animals except for their own domestic pets. Without the exposure provided by zoos and aquariums very few people would even care about the plight of animals in the wild, endangered or not. That would make the animal rights activists' work harder. Even so, you will never be able to win this argument, and you may come to feel guilty or embarrassed about what you are doing.

Your work will be done when and where most people are at play. If you pursue this career you will often be working on evenings, weekends, and holidays. That is when people are available to come to the zoo. You may even have to work overnight. That is when many animals are most active. Depending upon the exact nature of your job you may be needed most when the animals are up and about.

While a career in zoos or aquariums may be personally and professionally satisfying in many ways, you are unlikely to make much money in it. Top administrators and veterinarians may earn six figure salaries but nobody else does. Relatively few highly paid directors are required, but many workers with pretty ordinary paychecks are needed. Money can be one of your considerations when you choose a career, but only one. Many other factors, like professional fulfillment and providing an essential service, are much more important.

EDUCATION PATHWAYS

SEVERAL ACADEMIC PATHS WILL SET you up for a career in zoos or aquariums. There are a few specialized degree programs in zoo and aquarium administration that are specifically relevant to your goals. There is also the veterinarian route. There is the zoology path. The tough part may be choosing the one that's right for you.

You do not need a college degree to get started in this line of work. In fact, many very happy zoo and aquarium employees started out as summer workers while they were still in high school and never left.

There is no denying that you will go much farther with a college degree or even a master's degree. The zoo and aquarium field attracts many smart, committed people who devote their lives to their calling. Many people have graduate degrees. Scientists and veterinarians are common.

The obvious choices for undergraduate degrees are zoology or ichthyology, which are the studies of animals and fish, and how they live. There is also marine biology, which is about saltwater fish and habitats. These are all different from veterinary science, which is animal medicine. Zoos and aquariums definitely employ veterinarians. An undergraduate degree in zoology, marine biology or ichthyology, however, will get you started. A master's degree may become a necessity later in your career. Depending upon your career choices, however, an advanced degree in parks and recreation, business administration or something else entirely may be more appropriate. You don't have to make this decision any time soon. Let your career find its way for a while first.

Another option is to earn a specialized degree or certificate in zoo and aquarium administration. Degrees are available at the associate, bachelor's and master's levels, and are often offered in conjunction with zoos, aquariums or scientific programs. Certificates are at the postgraduate level, which means you have to possess a bachelor's degree in order to be eligible for one. Academic credentials in zoo and aquarium administration tend to be interdisciplinary programs that combine coursework from zoology, business administration, and parks and recreation programs. Everybody gets into this work because they care about animals, which makes the zoology courses necessary. If you want to succeed, however, you need to know something about running a business. The business model favored by zoos and aquariums is very similar to that of theme parks, which brings the parks and recreation courses into the picture. If a high-ranking position at a zoo or aquarium is your goal you can't go wrong by earning one of these degrees or certificates.

No matter which academic path you choose you cannot get through your college years without completing an internship. An internship is a job related to your major field of study that takes the place of regular classes for a summer or semester. Most internships are paid, and many come with advanced training not available to a company's regular employees. Every zoo and aquarium in the country hires interns. They are enthusiastic, eager to learn and, compared to regular employees, inexpensive. Never again in your life will you have the opportunity to try a career for a few months and then just leave if you decide it's not right for you. You will get valuable experience and make connections you can't make any other way. In fact, it's common for recent college graduates to get their first full-time jobs with an employer where they interned.

No matter which route you take to get started on your career you will never really be done with your education. Zoos and aquariums must constantly adapt to changing expectations by the public, new scientific discoveries, evolving laws and regulations, and numerable other variables that make it absolutely necessary that you be willing to be a lifelong learner. After you've earned a degree, you will get started on a lifetime of certificates and diplomas.

EARNINGS

NOBODY GETS RICH IN THE ZOO OR aquarium business. Opportunities for entrepreneurship are few, and most zoos and aquariums are not-for-profit organizations on a constant hunt for grants and donations to make ends meet.

You can, however, earn a perfectly respectable middle-class living doing something you love to do. Junior zookeepers with relatively little seniority and a bachelor's degree can earn from $35,000 to $40,000 per year. Curators, senior zookeepers who have moved into managerial positions, can earn $50,000 to $70,000 per year. A select few at very large, prestigious zoos and aquariums can break into six figures per year. There aren't very many of these positions but there's no reason you can't work your way up to one.

There are many positions within the field that lie between zookeepers and curators. Veterinarians, for example, can earn $60,000 to $80,000 per year. Careerists taking a scientific path as wildlife biologists or zoologists can earn $50,000 to $70,000 per year. Positions that don't directly involve working with animals but that are still critical to the overall functioning of a zoo or aquarium, like volunteer coordinators, typically pay $30,000 to $40,000 per year.

Keep in mind that earnings will vary somewhat in different parts of the country in keeping with the local cost of living. There are also some narrowly focused careers that are not so easily categorized, like marine-mammal trainers who work at aquaparks. Some small zoos and aquariums barely squeak by financially, while others, the largest and most prestigious, can afford to pay their people much better. You will probably start your career at one of the smaller institutions and work your way up to one of the larger ones.

Also remember that money wasn't one of the things that attracted you to this career. You have a sincere passion for animals and conservation. You are excited by the prospect of doing something for a living that most people only get to do for fun. You may have opportunities for travel and scientific discovery. You'll meet like-minded people and spend your days making your zoo and aquarium guests happy. That's a pretty good package.

OPPORTUNITIES

THERE IS NO SHORTAGE OF WAYS FOR you to get started on your career in zoos or aquariums while you are still in college. Nothing will prepare you for your career better than a part-time job at a zoo or aquarium. Just like park districts, theme parks and other attractions whose peak seasons are in the summer, zoos and aquariums hire thousands of college students every year. Those jobs can be full time over the summer, and some can morph into part-time jobs during the school year. You may be working in the gift shop or selling refreshments to tourists, but you'll get firsthand experience in how zoos and aquariums actually function. Gift shops and food vendors are actually essential sources of revenue for zoos and aquariums, most of which are not-for-profit enterprises. If you're lucky you may land a part-time job that deals directly with animals. But you'll learn something from anything you do.

Volunteering doesn't come with a paycheck but it does come with perks you can't get from a job that does – flexibility, for one. Part-time employees have serious responsibilities and are expected to do specific jobs at specific times. Volunteers can change their schedules at short notice and have relatively few actual responsibilities. Volunteers are also rotated frequently, which will give you exposure to different departments within the organization. Volunteering is such an important part of running zoos and aquariums – and many other not-for-profit institutions – that you owe it to yourself to find out how it really works. You could be a volunteer administrator someday. Volunteering may lack the intensity and structure of actual employment but it's a great way to learn about the operation.

Travel has never been easier or cheaper than it is today. Deals and discounts aimed at college students can make it even cheaper. Seize the moment and do some serious traveling to see animals up close and personal in their natural habitats. Go climbing in the Rockies, hiking in Alaska and on a photo safari in Kenya. These are all less expensive than you probably think, especially if you are willing to rough it, backpacking or camping. The popularity of ecotourism and adventure travel has created thousands of options for eco-minded travelers to learn more about wildlife and the remote corners of the world.

GETTING STARTED

WHEN THE TIME HAS COME TO GET your first full-time job at a zoo or aquarium, don't put it off. Part-time jobs in this field are pretty easy to get. It's the full-time, career-oriented jobs that are more difficult to come by. If you already have a part-time job when you finish college, see if you can turn it into a full-time job. It may not happen right away, and you may not stay in the same position. Just make it known to your employer that you are available for the next full-time position that opens up at your level. You might be surprised at the reaction you get. Hiring people from the outside costs money. Promoting somebody from within is easier and less expensive. Your goal at this stage is to tell the world you're serious about your career by turning your fun, part-time job into a serious, full-time job.

If you can't take this route, don't worry. If you have completed at least one internship or did some volunteering while you were in school you should have a long list of connections in the business, so get in touch with them. Email your résumé far and wide. Follow up with telephone calls. Don't hesitate to make a few visits. Your connections can be an invaluable resource. If the first person you call doesn't have anything available right at the moment, they may know of somebody who does. The community of zoo and aquarium professionals is a small one, and people move around as projects and grants migrate from one facility to the next. A handful of good connections could get you farther than you think.

Whatever you do, don't lose heart and don't be too picky about your first job in the business. Your goal is to separate yourself from the herd of part-timers, and make it clear that you are in this profession for the long haul. Your previous work history and academic credentials will back you up. You'll learn something useful from whatever job you get, so don't worry about it. Once you're in, you'll have a much easier time making connections and finding out what opportunities are available and where.

ASSOCIATIONS, PERIODICALS, WEBSITES

☐**African Association of Zoos and Aquaria**
www.paazab.com

☐**Alliance of Marine Mammal Parks and Aquariums**
www.ammpa.org

☐**American Association of Zoo Keepers**
www.aazk.org

☐**American Association of Zoo Veterinarians**
www.aazv.org

☐**Animal Behavior Management Alliance**
www.theabma.org

☐**Aquarium and Zoos Facilities Association**
www.azfa.org

☐**Aquarium Fish International**
www.fishchannel.com/affc_portal.aspx

☐Association of Zoo and Aquarium Docents
www.azadocents.org

☐Association of Zoo and Aquarium Volunteer
Administrators
www.rollinghillswildlife.com
/vol_web/index.html

☐Association of Zoo Veterinary Technicians
www.azvt.org

☐Association of Zoological Horticulture
www.azh.org

☐Association of Zoos and Aquariums
www.aza.org

☐Chicago Zoological Society
www.czs.org/czs/home.aspx

☐Disney's Animal Kingdom Park
www.disneyworld.disney.go.com
/parks/animal-kingdom/

☐European Association of Zoos and Aquaria
www.eaza.net

☐Freshwater and Marine Aquarium
www.fishchannel.com/fama_portal.aspx

☐Frozen Ark
www.frozenark.org

☐George Mason University
http://mais.gmu.edu/concentrations
/show/LA-MAIS-ISIN-ZAL

☐Good Zoo Guide
www.goodzoos.com

☐International Aquarium Forum
www.intaquaforum.org

☐International Animal Data Information Systems Committee
www.iadisc.org

☐International Association of Amusement Parks and Attractions
www.iaapa.org

☐International Association of Avian Trainers and Educators
www.iaate.org

☐International Marine Animal Trainers Association
www.imata.org

☐International Species Information System
www.isis.org

☐International Zoo Educators Association
www.izea.net

☐Jefferson Community College
www.sunyjefferson.edu/amg
/amg_facilities.html

☐Lincoln Park Zoo
www.lpzoo.com

☐Michigan State University
www.msu.edu

☐Ocean Project
www.theoceanproject.org

☐Oregon Coast Community College
www.occc.cc.or.us/aquarium/faq.html

☐San Diego Zoo
www.sandiegozoo.org

☐Santa Fe College
www.sfcollege.edu/zoo

☐SeaWorld
www.seaworld.com

☐Smithsonian National Zoological Park
www.nationalzoo.org

☐Tropical Fish Hobbyist
www.tfhmagazine.com

☐Western Illinois University
www.wiu.edu/GRAD/catalog
/zooaquastudies.php

☐Wildlife Information Network
www.wildlifeinformation.org

☐World Association of Zoos and Aquariums
www.waza.org

☐World Wide Zoo Net
http://library.thinkquest.org/3378
/index.html

☐Zoological Registrars Association
www.zooregistrars.org

☐Zoological Science
www.jstage.jst.go.jp/browse/zsj

☐ZooLex Zoo Design Organization
www.zoolex.org

☐Zoo Outreach Organization
www.zooreach.org

☐Zoos of the World
www.zoos.org